LEEDS BUSES SINCE 2000

KEITH A. JENKINSON

AMBERLEY

First published 2023

Amberley Publishing
The Hill, Stroud
Gloucestershire, GL5 4EP

www.amberley-books.com

Copyright © Keith A. Jenkinson, 2023

The right of Keith A. Jenkinson to be identified
as the Author of this work has been asserted in
accordance with the Copyrights, Designs and
Patents Act 1988.

ISBN 978 1 3981 0221 7 (print)
ISBN 978 1 3981 0222 4 (ebook)

British Library Cataloguing in Publication Data.
A catalogue record for this book is available from
the British Library.

Origination by Amberley Publishing.
Printed in the UK.

Buses in Leeds in the New Millennium

Public transport in Leeds has undergone numerous changes since the start of the new millennium, with many of the newcomers that flooded the city soon after deregulation having left the scene as a result of ceasing trading or having been swallowed up by the larger operators. While a few such as Black Prince, Optional Bus, and Geldards survived into the 2000s and others made their debut, Leeds is now mainly the preserve of FirstBus and Arriva, and to a lesser extent Transdev, who enter the city from Harrogate, Keighley and North Yorkshire.

Following the opening of the city's first guided busway – four sections in Scott Hall Road – in 1995, a second guideway was constructed – in three sections – on York Road in 2001, the latter bringing back memories of the trams that operated until the system's closure on 7 November 1959 on a reserve track in the centre of the road. While the Scott Hall Road guideway is used solely by First Leeds, that on York Road is shared by First Leeds and Arriva Yorkshire. Meanwhile, bendibuses made their debut in Leeds in June 1999 when First Leeds placed a number of Wright-bodied Volvo B10LAs in service and added some Wright-bodied Volvo B7LAs in April 2000. Later, in February 2007 First introduced its revolutionary Wrightbus 'ftr' Volvo B7LAs on a cross-city route from Pudsey to Seacroft and five years later, after gaining those previously operated by First York, introduced them on the intercity Leeds to Bradford service. Ultimately, however, bendibus operation in the city ceased in 2016.

Before the last century closed, in 1991 West Yorkshire Passenger Transport Authority drew up plans to reintroduce trams to the city, but as a result of failing to gain government backing, these were abandoned in 2005. However, still determined to bring electric transport back, in 2010 it submitted plans for a trolleybus system, but these again failed when in 2016 the government refused to provide the necessary funding. Still refusing defeat, in 2018 West Yorkshire Combined Authority drew up yet another proposal, this time to create a mass rapid transport system within the city that, if accepted would open in 2033, but at the time of writing it is not known whether or not this will come to fruition.

Meanwhile, although First Leeds purchased a sizeable number of new buses, it also received a number of older vehicles – largely double-deckers – from the group's other subsidiaries across the UK, while in 2011 it bought its first hybrid buses, sixteen Wright-bodied Volvo B5LHs, which were painted in a special livery to indicate their propulsion. A few years earlier, route branding was added to a number of buses wearing the standard corporate First livery and this was progressively altered as time moved on, and in 2013 the bold new Leeds skyline fleet name began to be applied. Then, towards the end of 2018 the logo and livery changed again on a number of buses when the Leedscity fleet name appeared on the new Wrightbus StreetDecks, which wore a new two-tone green scheme to which a range of different route colours was applied to the upper front deck. However, after a few years the route colours were replaced with standard dark green paintwork.

In June 2014 West Yorkshire Combined Authority opened its first dedicated park and ride site at Elland Road close to Leeds United Football Club's stadium, and for its operation a number of Wright-bodied Volvo B9TLs were employed wearing an all-over dedicated livery. Following this, a second park and ride site was opened at Temple Green in 2017, being maintained with new dedicated liveried micro hybrid Wrightbus StreetDeck HEVs (which also replaced the Volvo B5LHs on the Elland Road operation), and then in 2021 a third park & ride was commissioned at Stourton, employing BYD-Alexander Dennis pure electric double-deckers. Previously, in the autumn of 2020 First Leeds had placed nine Yutong E10 all-electric single-deckers in service wearing a distinctive bright green livery.

Moving on to the other operators whose buses were to be seen in the city, Arriva initially used its standard aquamarine and Cotswold Stone 'cow horn' and swept front liveries and then in 2009 it adopted an interurban style based on two shades of blue that in 2020 was replaced by overall light blue with a white diagonal band. In 2013, a new green and blue colour scheme and lettering appeared on its hybrid Wright-bodied Volvo B5LHs (which was changed in 2022) while a two-tone blue scheme was used on its 'Max' and 'Sapphire' buses upon which route branding was also applied. Prior to this, Yorkshire Traction operated the services from Huddersfield as well as from Barnsley and after the company was purchased by Stagecoach in December 2005 those from Huddersfield ultimately passed to Arriva Yorkshire. The service from Barnsley, however, remained with Stagecoach Yorkshire and after being replaced by an half-hourly limited stop route in 2017, as a result of the coronavirus pandemic, it was reduced to two journeys per day. Stagecoach also operated an express service from Hull to Leeds via the M62 motorway and although this was discontinued in 2020 as a consequence of the pandemic, it was later restarted, albeit by two return daily Megabus journeys. In addition, Stagecoach Megabus operates into Leeds from a number of other destinations across the UK.

Also coming into the city from other towns is Transdev, whose Keighley Bus Company buses were to be seen in a variety of liveries and Harrogate Bus Company's vehicles in various red and cream, red and maroon and red and black colour schemes, most of which carried branding. In addition, Transdev's blue and cream-liveried Coastliner buses entered the bus station from York and some North Yorkshire towns as well Transdev York's CityZap express service from its home city, and also from Leeds Bradford Airport on the Flyer service that had been gained from Yorkshire Tiger in September 2020. Due, however, to falling passenger numbers following covid, CityZap was discontinued from 19 November 2022 and the buses operating it were then rebranded and transferred to the Leeds to Wetherby X98 and X99 services. Prior to all this, Transdev Coastliner in conjunction with City Sightseeing had launched a summer months open-top Leeds tour on 25 May 2010 using a pair of former London MCW Metrobuses, but perhaps unsurprisingly in a city with few architectural delights or areas of interest, this did not prove popular and was not repeated after 2011.

In addition to the major operators, Leeds has also seen several independent operators having a presence in the city, some of which were already there in 2000 while others made their debut during the next two decades. Of those who had entered the fray in the twentieth century following deregulation, Optional Bus, Horsforth (owned jointly by J&B Travel and Hunters Coaches) sold its local bus services to First Leeds in 2001 but continued their individual coaching and school bus operations; Guiseley-based Aztecbird, who had maintained the service to Leeds Bradford Airport since 1998, ceased trading in 2004; Black Prince of Morley, together with its associated Suburban Buses and Leeds City Transport, continued its operations until July 2005 when it sold out to FirstBus; and Leeds-based Geldards Coaches, who had started in 1991, disappeared from the scene in September 2015 when it went into liquidation.

Just as the above disappeared, others made their debut in the city with new commercially registered services and others gained through the tendering process. The first of these was Halifax Joint Committee, who registered a route from Portsmouth (in Calderdale) to Leeds in March 2000 and after truncating it to Halifax continued it until June 2002. Added to this on May 2001 was an infrequent service from Bradford, which was basically for vehicle positioning journeys. In 2006 HCT Group CT Plus entered the city operating schools services and, later, in May 2019 gained its first local bus services in the city before suddenly ceasing trading on 5 August 2022 and going into administration. Meanwhile, Yorkshire Traction's services from Huddersfield to Leeds had passed to Arriva while the company itself was acquired by Stagecoach, who in May 2008 sold its Huddersfield depot's buses and operations to Centrebus Holdings Ltd, a company set up by Leicester-based Centrebus (60 per cent) and Arriva (40 per cent). After operating as White Rose Bus Company under the Centrebus name and livery, and gaining a number of tendered local bus services in Leeds in 2010, Centrebus sold its share to Arriva in September 2013, who rebranded it as Yorkshire Tiger and continued to operate the tendered services in Leeds until it ultimately lost all of them except the Leeds Bradford Airport route, which it passed to Transdev on 30 August 2020.

Making its appearance in the city in October 2018, when it started a half-hourly service to Aberford in competition against First Leeds, was independent Harrogate Coach Travel of Tockwith, who traded as Connexionsbuses. Also entering the fray, albeit briefly, was old established leisure company Fourway Coaches, who began a tendered park & ride service from Woodhouse Lane to the city centre, operating it from April to June 2002. Much later, in December 2015 following the cancellation of a bus service from Horsforth to Pudsey, Fourway Coaches launched a service in the Leeds suburbs between these two points on a fifteen-month contract, but then reverted back to its old established coach operations. Then came Yeadon-based Pegasus.com, who gained the tenders for some services in Aireborough and Otley but returned to its coaching activities in 2007. Another newcomer was Square Peg Buses, who began in 2014 operating a number of school services and later entered the local bus market with a handful of services, all of which covered suburban areas and did not enter the city centre, while Batley-based Hawkins, who traded as Station Coaches, extended its Ossett to Wakefield service into Leeds central bus station and continues this in 2022. Following the collapse of CT Plus (Yorkshire) on 5 August, its 81 service (Leeds–Pudsey) was taken over, albeit on a reduced timetable, by Square Peg, while on 19 September Tockwith-based A&A Buses made its debut into the Leeds area when it began operating the local Horsforth 30 route. On 3 October yet another new operator arrived when newly formed five-bus Yorkshire Travel Group began a local city service and followed it with a second one on 7 November.

In addition to the above, several coach operators around Leeds added school bus operations around the suburbs to their leisure market activities, and some also frequently operated rail replacement services when these were necessary. Among these were Stanningley-based J&B Travel and Hunters Coaches, who as mentioned earlier had operated Optional Bus, Kilvington of Pudsey, and Tetleys Motor Services, Leeds, who all possessed double-deckers for these duties, as too did the previously mentioned CT Plus. In addition to all the above, the coaches of Wallace Arnold, whose headquarters were in Leeds, were also regularly seen passing through the city centre on private hire or tours duties until 2007 when their name was replaced by Shearings, who had acquired the company two years earlier.

Finally, as was to be expected, a city as large as Leeds is served by express services from across the country provided by National Express and Megabus while Flixbus can now also regularly be seen and coaches contracted to Bus Eireann also make appearances on Eurolines services.

With so many changes having taken place in Leeds since 2000, unfortunately it has not been possible to include every single one within ninety-six pages, but I have tried to cover as many as space allowed and hope this is found acceptable. While most of the photographs have been taken by myself, without the help of others there would have been a few gaps and I thus thank those who have allowed me to fill them with their work. Additionally, the photographers of some of those provided through friend's collections are unknown, and to these I sincerely apologise, but hope they are nevertheless happy to see their pictures in print.

The first bendibuses to operate in Leeds were Wright-bodied Volvo B10LA's introduced by First Leeds in the summer of 1999. One of these, 1109 (T109 VWU), which entered service in August of that year, is pictured here in 2000 approaching Holt Park shopping centre on the outskirts of Leeds carrying route branding for cross-city route 1 to Beeston on its cove panels. (K. A. Jenkinson)

The largest coach operator in Leeds for several decades was independently owned Wallace Arnold, who ultimately merged with Shearings in 2005. Typifying the fleet at the beginning of the new millennium is Volvo B10M R416 FWT, which carries a Plaxton Premier 350 body. (T. W. W. Knowles)

Seen at their owners Geldard Coaches' depot in 2000 are Van Hool-bodied DAF GDZ 9114, which was new in January 1986, and Scania XXI 8968, which began life in September 1985. (Author's collection)

Still wearing the corporate livery of its former owner, Stagecoach Manchester, Northern Counties-bodied Scania BR112DH FWH 462Y, which was new to Greater Manchester PTE in March 1983, is seen here operated by Black Prince, Morley, on its Bradford to Crossgates service in early 2000. (K. A. Jenkinson)

Alexander-bodied Scania N113DRB J810 HMC, which started life with East London in October 1991 and passed to MTL, Liverpool, before reaching Black Prince, Morley, is seen here in Park Row, Leeds, operating the 63B service to the city's university. (Barry Newsome)

Black Prince, Morley, associate Leeds Suburban Buses ex-Newport Transport Marshall-bodied Scania BR112DH 97 (PTG 97Y), which was new in January 1983, is seen here at its depot with a former London Transport MetroScania being used for spares standing in the background. (Barry Newsome collection)

Guiseley independent Aztecbird's Ikarus-bodied DAF SB220 YD02 RJJ, which had been purchased new in May 2002, heads off to Otley after calling at Leeds Bradford Airport from Leeds on the 757 service, for which it carries bold branding. (K. A. Jenkinson)

New to Maidstone & District in April 1984, MCW Metrobus A210 OKJ is pictured here wearing an all-over advertising livery at the depot of its owner, Horsforth independent J&B Coaches, in 2001. (K. A. Jenkinson)

Originating with Yorkshire Coastliner in February 1995, coach-seated Alexander-bodied Volvo Olympian 925 (M925 UYG) is seen on 4 May 2001 after being transferred to Keighley & District wearing branding for the Keighley to Leeds AireLink 760 service. (T. M. Leach)

Arriva Yorkshire's seventeen-month-old Plaxton-bodied Dennis Dart SLF 228 (V228 PCX), which carries small 'easy' branding above its front wheel arch, heads through Leeds city centre en route to Castleford on 3 May 2000. (K. A. Jenkinson)

New to Yorkshire Rider in October 1990, First Leeds Northern Counties-bodied Scania N113DRC 8008 (H808 TWX), wearing the faded step-entrance style barbie livery, makes its way through Rawdon on the 736 service to Leeds on 28 April 2001. (K. A. Jenkinson)

Seen in First Leeds Kirkstall depot on its new advert launch day, 3 May 2001, is fourteen-month-old Alexander-bodied Volvo B7TL 5701 (W701 CWR), which was covered with a Contra Vision map showing First's Overground routes and fares offers across the city's network. (K. A. Jenkinson)

One of two Harrogate & District coach-seated Alexander-bodied Volvo Olympians painted in this version of the branding for the Leeds to Ripon 36 service, 408 (L8 YCL), which began life with Yorkshire Coastliner in October 1983, is seen here in Chapeltown, Leeds, on 12 January 2001. (K. A. Jenkinson)

New to London Buses in March 1985 in dual-door format, MCW Metrobus B217 WUL was acquired by independent Halifax Joint Committee in October 2000 and converted to single-door before its entry into service. Here it is seen, freshly repainted, on its owner's 509 service from Halifax to Leeds on 15 April 2002. (K. A. Jenkinson)

Fitted with guide wheels, First Leeds Wright-bodied Scania L94UB 8131 (T431 GUG) is seen here en route to Aberford on the York Road guided busway followed by another First Leeds Scania L94UB and an Arriva Volvo B7TL on 12 January 2002. (K. A. Jenkinson)

Heading towards Leeds on the York Road guided busway on 12 January 2002 is Arriva Yorkshire Alexander-bodied Volvo B7TL 658 (W658 CWX), which carries route branding on its lower side panels for the four services from Castleford to Leeds and 'Elite' branding at the side of its destination screen. (K. A. Jenkinson)

Heading along Scott Hall Road on Leeds' first guided busway is First Leeds Wright Axcess-ultralow-bodied Scania L113CRL 8463 (R463 JFS). (K. A. Jenkinson)

New in November 1993 as a demonstrator for Optare, whose Vecta body is mounted on a MAN 11.190 chassis. Originally registered L834 MWT, after spending a few years with Seamarks, Luton, it was acquired by Guiseley independent Aztecbird, who reregistered it WPT 456. Here it is seen on 31 August 2002 heading through Rawdon to Leeds Bradford Airport on the 757 service from Leeds for which it carried branding. (K. A. Jenkinson)

Having disgraced itself, one of First Leeds Wright Axcess-ultralow-bodied Scania L113CRLs, used on the Superbus service along Scott Hall Road guided busway, heads through City Square, Leeds, on tow to Kirkstall depot behind 9404 (CJX 835Y), its owner's DAF 2500 recovery wagon, which was new in April 1983. (K. A. Jenkinson)

Making its way to Leeds on the York Road guided busway on the turquoise line 56 service on 12 January 2002, followed by one of its sisters, is First Leeds Alexander-bodied Volvo B7TL 5791 (X357 VWT) with 'Elite' branding on its destination screen. (K. A. Jenkinson)

Starting life with London Buses in January 1988, MCW Metrorider E643 KYW is seen here at Leeds Corn Exchange after being acquired by Optional Bus, Horsforth, who numbered it 4643. (Author's collection)

Both emigrating from the capital and seen here wearing First Leeds' corporate step-entry barbie livery are former Walthamstow Citybus all-Leyland Olympian 30710 (J142 YRM) and ex-London United Alexander-bodied Volvo Olympian 31775 (R940 YOV) heading down Park Row in the city centre on 18 November 2003. (K. A. Jenkinson)

Retaining its centre door, First Leeds ex-London United Alexander-bodied Volvo Olympian 31772 (R937 YOV) passes the statue of the Black Prince, eldest son of King Edward III, in City Square, Leeds, on 20 November 2003. (K. A. Jenkinson)

Imported from Stagecoach Kenya in 1998, Megabus Duple MetSec-bodied Dennis Dragon 15180 (M680 MDB) is seen here on Wellington Street, Leeds, at the start of its cross-Pennines journey to Manchester on 5 December 2003. (K. A. Jenkinson)

Turning into Leeds bus station at the end of its journey from Scarborough on 2 December 2004 is Yorkshire Coastliner Alexander Royale-bodied Volvo Olympian 436 (W436 CWX), which carries route branding above and below its lower deck side windows. This bus later passed to First Eastern Counties. (K. A. Jenkinson)

New to Capital Citybus in London, First Leeds Northern Counties-bodied Dennis Arrow 30586 (P413 MTW) prepares to enter Leeds bus station on 2 December 2004. (K. A. Jenkinson)

Wearing branding above its lower deck side windows for the X6 Leeds to Huddersfield service, upon which it is seen here on 23 April 2004, is First Bradford Alexander ALX400-bodied Volvo B7TL 30893 (W748 DWX). (K. A. Jenkinson)

Despite carrying side branding for the cross-city 16/16A services from Farsley to Seacroft, and Overground lettering below its cab window, First Leeds Alexander-bodied Volvo B7TL 30920 (W787 KBT) is pictured here on 23 April 2004 operating the intercity 72 service from Leeds to Bradford. (K. A. Jenkinson)

Delivered new to West Yorkshire PTE in November 1982, Roe-bodied Leyland Olympian 30601 (CUB 37Y) ended its days with First Leeds as a driver trainer and is seen here passing through City Square, Leeds, on 2 December 2004. (K. A. Jenkinson)

Painted in First's step-entrance version of its corporate 'barbie' livery, First Leeds dual-door Alexander (Belfast)-bodied Volvo Olympian 31760 (R921 WOE), which began life with London's Stanwell Buses in November 1997, is seen here travelling down Harrogate Road, Rawdon, en route to Leeds on 18 April 2004. (K. A. Jenkinson)

Originating with Sheffield Mainline in January 1996, Plaxton-bodied Mercedes Benz 709D 50183 (N116 DWE) is seen here turning from Boar Lane into Vicar Lane while operating a mobility bus service with First Leeds on 2 December 2004. (K. A. Jenkinson)

On loan to Arriva Yorkshire from Arriva Derby, and seen here in City Square, Leeds, on 2 December 2004, is Northern Counties-bodied Volvo Olympian 4626 (R626 MNU), which displays branding for two services in its rightful home. (K. A. Jenkinson)

New to Yorkshire Woollen District Transport in October 1991, Arriva Yorkshire's Leyland Lynx 2 372 (J372 AWT) stands in City Square, Leeds, awaiting its departure to Castleford on 10 December 2004. (K. A. Jenkinson)

Morley independent Black Prince's Leeds City Transport-liveried Alexander RH-bodied Scania N113DRB 238 (H238 LOM), which had started life with West Midlands Travel in November 1990, is seen here travelling down Woodhouse Lane, Leeds, en route to the city centre on 6 July 2004. (K. A. Jenkinson)

Starting life as a demonstrator in March 1989 before being purchased by Nottingham City Transport, Black Prince of Morley's Alexander RH-bodied Scania N113DRB 380 (F380 JTV) is seen here in Vicar Lane, Leeds, about to cross The Headrow on 28 July 2005, two days before the company was taken over by First Leeds. (K. A. Jenkinson)

Built in June 1984 for London Buses AVE trials, Alexander-bodied dual-door, twin staircase Ailsa B55 V3 (A103 SUU) suffered severe accident damage in 1992 and was then purchased in that condition by Black Prince, Morley, who slowly, and superbly, rebuilt it in single-door configuration. Here it is seen on Vicar Lane, Leeds, crossing The Headrow on an extremely wet 28 July 2005. (K. A. Jenkinson)

Making their way along Vicar Lane, Leeds, on 28 April 2005 are First Leeds Wright-bodied Scania L113CRL 61063 (R449 JSG) and Black Prince ex-London Northern Alexander-bodied Scania N113DRB 421 (F421 GNG), which, although seen here on the 54 service to Morley, wore the blue and cream livery introduced for operation on the former Amberley Travel service from Leeds to Bradford. (K. A. Jenkinson)

New to independent Geldards Bigfoot Buses, Leeds, in April 1997 and registered P2 BFB, then purchased by Black Prince in 1998 and reregistered P818 AWT, this East Lancs Flyte-bodied Scania L113CRL passed to First Leeds along with the Morley-based company in July 2005. Here it is seen still in its former owner's livery after receiving its new custodian's fleet names. (Neil Halliday's collection)

Another bus to pass to First Leeds together with Black Prince's business on 30 July 2005, Alexander RH-bodied Scania N113DRB F428 GWG was new to London Northern in July 1989 and then passed to MTL, Liverpool, before reaching Morley. Pictured here numbered 36928 by its new owner and displaying its identity, it still retains Black Prince's 2004 livery commemorating its thirty-fifth anniversary. (Neil Halliday's collection)

Seen on 11 June 2005 on Purple Line service 49, Wright Gemini-bodied Volvo B7TL 32473 (YJ04 FZZ) displays First Leeds' early style of route branding, which was applied below its lower deck windows. (K. A. Jenkinson)

Originating with London Northern in November 1995 registered N417 KBV, after its acquisition by Yorkshire Traction, who ultimately reregistered it YTC 838, the Northern Counties-bodied Volvo Olympian is seen here on a damp July day in 2005 heading along Vicar Lane, Leeds, on its way to Huddersfield. (K. A. Jenkinson)

Departing Leeds Bradford Airport on a 757 journey to Leeds on 1 March 2007 is First Leeds Wright-bodied Volvo B7RLE 66702 (YK53 GXL), which carries appropriate route, and other, branding above and below its windows. (K. A. Jenkinson)

Standing at their depot on 6 September 2006 are Yeadon-based independent Pegasus.com's Plaxton-bodied Leyland Tiger H267 GRY, which was new to Barfordian, Plaxton-bodied Dennis Dart SLF V270 BNV, which began life with Tellings Golden Miller, and the company's support van. (K. A. Jenkinson)

Standing at the Pudsey terminus of route 4 from Seacroft on 2 March 2007 is First Leeds 'ftr'-liveried Wright-bodied Volvo B7LA street car 19013 (YJ06 XLS), still featuring a cover on its front wheel, which was fitted from new. (K. A. Jenkinson)

Seen at Leeds rail station operated by First Leeds on the free Leeds Citybus service on 15 August 2007 is West Yorkshire Metro (PTE)-owned Optare Solo M950SL 53909 (YJ07 EHR) wearing Metro Connect livery and branding for this service. (K. A. Jenkinson)

New to Hughes-DAF, Gomersal, in June 1997 and used as a demonstrator, Northern Counties-bodied originally LPG-powered DAF SB220 P10 LPG is seen leaving Leeds rail station on 15 August 2007 after being sold to Arriva Yorkshire, who gave it fleet number 435 and converted it to conventional diesel power. (K. A. Jenkinson)

Devoid of all forms of identity, Arriva Yorkshire Alexander ALX400-bodied Volvo B7TL 651 (W651 CWX), which joined the company new in April 2000, passes through City Square, Leeds, on a journey to Castleford on 15 August 2007. (K. A. Jenkinson)

Caught by the camera in City Square, Leeds, on 15 August 2007, First Leeds Alexander-bodied Scania N113CRB 61090 (K612 HUG) was new to Yorkshire Rider in April 1993. (K. A. Jenkinson)

Standing in Wellington Street, Leeds, collecting its London-bound passengers on 16 September 2007, Megabus.com Plaxton-bodied Volvo B10M 52310 (N619 USS) started life in Scotland with Stagecoach Bluebird in September 1995. (K. A. Jenkinson)

Picking up its passengers at Leeds rail station on 16 September 2007 while operating a rail replacement service is Bova FHD12 Y716 SUB, which was new to Fraser Eagle, Accrington, in July 2001 but is lettered with its subsidiary Tyrer Tours fleet name. (K. A. Jenkinson)

Awaiting its next rail replacement duty at Leeds rail station on 16 September 2007 is Horsforth-based JB Travel's Hispano-bodied Mercedes Benz 0404 J995 TOJ, which began life with Clarkston, South Elmsall, in March 2001. Behind it is Godsons, Leeds, Plaxton Panther-bodied Iveco Eurorider YN05 VRY, which was also on rail replacement duties. (K. A. Jenkinson)

Although Fraser Eagle held the contract for the rail replacement services from Leeds on 16 September 2007, as was customary it hired coaches from several other operators. Here, however, seen on this work on Infirmary Street, Leeds, is one of its own coaches – Van Hool-bodied DAF SB4000 YJ04 BYB. (K. A. Jenkinson)

Standing in the yard of First Leeds' Kirkstall depot on 16 September 2007 showing the two variants of First's corporate livery are a Plaxton-bodied Dennis Dart, two ex-London Stanwell Buses Alexander (Belfast)-bodied Volvo Olympians, and two Wright Gemini-bodied Volvo B7TLs, which were new to First Leeds. (K. A. Jenkinson)

Appearing earlier in the book, First Leeds ex-Geldards and Black Prince East Lancs Flyte-bodied Scania L113CRL 64808 (P818 AWT) is seen here on 19 February 2008 in First's corporate livery making its way up Bishopgate Street towards City Square, Leeds. (K. A. Jenkinson)

One of several buses painted in the attractive Unilink livery for operation on the service from the city centre to its two universities, First Leeds dual-door Alexander (Belfast)-bodied Volvo Olympian 31765 (R926 WOE), seen here on Boar Lane on 19 February 2008, began life in London with Stanwell Buses in December 1997. (K. A. Jenkinson)

Resting alongside its depot on 14 March 2008 is Horsforth independent coach operator Thornes Independent's Van Hool-bodied Volvo B12B VH02 OOH, which was new to Blackburn Coachlines in June 2002 registered PJ02 UXR. (K. A. Jenkinson)

Departing from Leeds bus station on 17 March 2009 is First Leeds Alexander Royale-bodied Volvo Olympian 31685 (P590 WSU), which had been transferred from First Glasgow, but had begun life with Strathclyde Buses in May 1997. (K. A. Jenkinson)

During the early 2000s First West Yorkshire had received numerous buses cascaded from other First Group subsidiaries. One such example, seen in Leeds bus station on 17 March 2009, was Northern Counties-bodied Volvo Olympian 34142 (L642 SEU), which had been acquired from First Bristol, to whom it was delivered new in November 1993. (K. A. Jenkinson)

Seen in Leeds bus station on 17 March 2009 is Alexander-bodied Scania L113CRL 61046 (M402 UUB), which had been transferred to First Leeds from Rider York where it had started its life in August 1994. (K. A. Jenkinson)

Branded for the 770 service from Leeds to Harrogate via Wetherby, and seen here in Leeds bus station on 17 March 2009, Transdev Harrogate & District Plaxton-bodied Volvo B7TL 2706 (Y706 HRN) was new in July 2001 and had originally been operated by Burnley & Pendle. (K. A. Jenkinson)

Purchased new by West Yorkshire Metro (PTE) in April 2007, Metro Connect-liveried Optare Solo M950SL 53908 (YJ07 EHP), seen here operated by First Leeds, departs from Leeds bus station on 17 March 2009 on the free Citybus service for which it carried branding. (K. A. Jenkinson)

First Leeds even received Optare Solos from other First Group subsidiaries, as illustrated by 53106 (EO02 FLF), which started life with First Essex in March 2002 and is seen here circumnavigating Eastgate roundabout, Leeds, on 17 March 2009. (K. A. Jenkinson)

Seen in Eastgate, Leeds, on the 229 service to Huddersfield in March 2009 is Arriva West Yorkshire's immaculately presented Alexander-bodied DAF SB220 460 (R460 KWT), which was already eleven years old. (K. A. Jenkinson)

Displaying route branding for the X84 service to Otley, Ilkley and Skipton, one-month-old First Leeds Wright Gemini-bodied Volvo B9TL 37670 (YJ58 RSY) makes its approach to Leeds bus station on 17 March 2009. (K. A. Jenkinson)

Nearing the end of its long journey from Bridlington on 17 March 2009 as it turns into St Peters Street from Eastgate, Leeds, is Transdev Yorkshire Coastliner Wright-bodied Volvo B7TL 407 (YK55 ATU). (K. A. Jenkinson)

New to Yorkshire Rider in June 1994, First Bradford Northern Counties-bodied Volvo Olympian 30755 (L402 PWR) has only a few yards remaining to reach its destination, Leeds bus station, at the end of its journey from Bradford on the 670 service on 17 March 2009. (K. A. Jenkinson)

Sparkling clean, nine-year-old First Leeds Alexander ALX400-bodied Volvo B7TL 30932 (X352 VWY) turns from Eastgate on to St Peters Street on the cross-Leeds 50 service to Seacroft on 17 March 2009. (K. A. Jenkinson)

Seen in Ilkley in March 2009 while being evaluated by First Leeds is thirteen-seat Koch-bodied Mercedes Benz 411CDI 54098 (LT02 NVB), which was new to First Capital, London, in March 2002. (T. M. Leach collection)

Awaiting its London-bound passengers in Kirkgate, Leeds, during the afternoon of 17 March 2009 is Megabus.com Jonckheere-bodied Volvo B10M 52659 (V909 DDY), which originated with Stagecoach East Kent in October 1999. (K. A. Jenkinson)

A much travelled coach, Hunters of Stanningley's Irizar Century-bodied Scania L94IB P3 HCL was first operated by Bus Eireaan registered 99-D-55050 in July 1999 before crossing to England and gaining registration number T409 OWA. It then passed to Hunters, who changed this to P3 HCL. Here it is seen passing through Leeds city centre in March 2009. (K. A. Jenkinson)

A busy scene on Vicar Lane, Leeds, on 17 March 2009 shows First Leeds ex-London United Alexander-bodied Volvo Olympian 31170 (R934 YOV), which had been converted from dual- to single-door layout, and First Leeds Alexander-bodied Volvo B7TL 30917 (W772 KBT). (K. A. Jenkinson)

Wearing branding for the 202/203 services from Leeds to Huddersfield and a strapline reading 'Connecting Kirklees', Arriva West Yorkshire East Lancs-bodied VDL DB250 1600 (YJ06 AYF) heads along Vicar Lane, Leeds, on 17 March 2009, followed by a First Leeds Wright-bodied Scania L113 CRL. (K. A. Jenkinson)

Seen on Vicar Lane, Leeds, on 17 March 2009 is First Leeds Wright Gemini-bodied Volvo B9TL 37108 (YK07 AYF), with multi-branding for Red Line routes 2, 3, and 3A and Blue Line 12, 13 and 13A on its side panels and front and side windows. It is followed by First Leeds Wright-bodied Volvo B7LA 'ftr' bendibus 19020 (YJ07 LVM). (K. A. Jenkinson)

Entering City Square, Leeds, from Park Row in 17 March 2009 is First Leeds Wright-bodied Volvo B10LA 10024 (T107 YWU), which carries branding for cross-city route 1 – Holt Park to Beeston – on the cove panels of its front module. (K. A. Jenkinson)

New to K-Line, Huddersfield, in October 1994, Arriva West Yorkshire Ikarus-bodied DAF SB220 22 (M812 RCP) is seen here in Pudsey bus station on the service to Dewsbury in March 2009 together with First Leeds Alexander-bodied Volvo Olympian 30245 (S661 NUG). (K. A. Jenkinson)

Dominating Eastgate, Leeds, on 17 March 2009 are elderly First Leeds all-Leyland Olympian 30720 (J148 YRM), which began life with Walthamstow Citybus in November 1991, First Leeds Wright-bodied Volvo B7TL 37030 (YJ06 XKV), and First Bradford Wright-bodied Volvo B9TL 37064 (YK57 EZT), which carries route branding for the 72 service to its home city. (K. A. Jenkinson)

Making its way through Leeds bus station in March 2009 is Arriva Fox County's National Express-liveried Van Hool Alizee-bodied VDL SB4000 3202 (YJ54 CFE), which was new in September 2004. (K. A. Jenkinson)

Heading along St Peters Street, Leeds, past the bus station on 17 March 2009, is Arriva West Yorkshire East Lancs-bodied Volvo Olympian 519 (M695 HPF), which started life with London & Country in October 1994. (K. A. Jenkinson)

Among the many second-hand buses to pass to First Leeds, Alexander (Belfast)-bodied Volvo Olympian 31815 (XDZ 5915) originated with Stanwell Buses, London, in October 1997, and is seen here leaving Leeds bus station on 25 March 2009. (K. A. Jenkinson)

Leaving Leeds bus station at the start of its 770 journey to Harrogate via Wetherby on 25 March 2009 is Transdev Harrogate & District Wright-bodied Volvo B10BLE 1085 (PO51 MTY), which was new to Lancashire United in December 2001. (K. A. Jenkinson)

Branded for the prestigious 36 service from Leeds to Ripon, Transdev Harrogate & District Wright Gemini-bodied Volvo B7TL 3607 (YC53 MXT) enters St Peters Street, Leeds, shortly before reaching the bus station on 25 March 2009. (K. A. Jenkinson)

Seen in Leeds city centre on 25 March 2009 is independent Geldards Optare Spectra-bodied DAF DB250 YJ51 ZVE, which had been acquired from Ensignbus, Purfleet, whose livery and fleet number it still carries, but was new to Reading Transport in November 2001. (K. A. Jenkinson)

With branding for route 110 and strapline 'Connecting Wakefield and Leeds', Arriva West Yorkshire East Lancs-bodied Volvo B9TL 1805 (YJ08 EEF) makes its way towards the exit of Leeds bus station on 25 March 2009. (K. A. Jenkinson)

Also leaving Leeds bus station on 25 March 2009 displaying branding for the 254 and 255 services and a 'Connecting Cleckheaton and Leeds' strapline on its side panels is Arriva West Yorkshire Wright-bodied Volvo B7RLE 1109 (YJ08 DVP), which was new in July 2008. (K. A. Jenkinson)

Starting life with Keighley & District in January 2001, and seen here approaching Leeds bus station at the end of its journey from its home town on 25 March 2009, is freshly repainted Wright Renown-bodied Volvo B10BLE 564 (X564 YUG). Later, after being transferred to Transdev Lancashire United, then Harrogate and York, it was sold to Isle Coaches, Owston Ferry, in 2014. (K. A. Jenkinson)

After exiting Leeds bus station, Transdev Keighley & District Northern Counties-bodied Volvo Olympian 988 (S58 VNM), which began life with London Sovereign in December 1998, turns into Eastgate at the start of its journey to Keighley on the 760 service on 25 March 2009. (K. A. Jenkinson)

New to Lincolnshire Road Car Co. in March 1998, Stagecoach Hull East Lancs-Pyoneer-bodied Volvo Olympian 16807 (R687 MFE) is seen in Leeds on 25 March 2009 operating the express X62 motorway service to its home city. (K. A. Jenkinson)

Wearing branding for the Huddersfield–Leeds–Bradford X6 service, First Bradford Wright Gemini-bodied Volvo B9TL 37079 (YJ08 CVP) is seen approaching Leeds bus station on 25 March 2009. (K. A. Jenkinson)

New to Yorkshire Rider in July 1994, First Leeds Alexander-bodied Scania L113CRL L655 PWR, displaying two fleet numbers – 50 and 61133 – is seen here on Vicar Lane, Leeds, on 25 March 2009 after being demoted to driver training duties. (K. A. Jenkinson)

Seen in City Square, Leeds, on 25 March 2009 are Arriva West Yorkshire Alexander-bodied DAF SB220 466 (S466 GUB) and Optare Spectra-bodied DAF DB250 640 (V640 KVH) wearing their owner's new and old liveries. (K. A. Jenkinson)

Displaying branding for the intercity Bradford to Leeds 72 service, and pictured here on 27 March 2009, is First Bradford Wright Gemini-bodied Volvo B9TL 37065 (YK57 EZU), which was later transferred to First York. (K. A. Jenkinson)

Wearing the livery of its previous owner, Menzies, Heathrow, and displaying an Airport Direct fleet name, Centrebus all-Scania CN94UB YN03 UVS departs from Leeds Bradford Airport on the tendered 757 service to Leeds on 26 April 2010. (K. A. Jenkinson)

Also leaving Leeds Bradford Airport on 26 April 2010, albeit on a commercially registered service 757 to Leeds, is First Leeds Wright Gemini-bodied Volvo B9TL 37699 (YJ09 OAS). (K. A. Jenkinson)

Heading along Leeds Road, Rawdon, on a school bus duty on 23 September 2010, is Stanningley independent JB Travel's Alexander-bodied Volvo Olympian J600 JBT, which started life registered N119 UHP with London United on Airbus duties in September 1995. (K. A. Jenkinson)

Owned by West Yorkshire Metro (PTE) but operated by CT Plus, Wakefield, BMC 220 BC026 (YJ56 ZTF) is seen at Leeds Bradford Airport, depositing a party of holiday-bound schoolchildren on 26 April 2010. (K. A. Jenkinson)

Arriving at the Royal Armouries Museum, Leeds, on 24 May 2010 while operating the city's unsuccessful sightseeing tour is Transdev Coastliner MCW Metrobus GYE 603W, which had started life with London Buses as a conventional closed top bus in August 1981, and was then converted to part open-top in 200. It was then sold to Top Line Travel, York, in April 2005, before moving to Transdev in 2008. (K. A. Jenkinson)

With Contra Vision advertising covering all its side windows on both decks, no doubt to the delight of its passengers, First Leeds Wright Gemini-bodied Volvo B9TL 37698 (YJ09 OAP) is seen here leaving Otley bus station on an X84 journey to Leeds on 23 September 2009. (K. A. Jenkinson)

Entering City Square, Leeds, from Infirmary Street on 9 January 2012 is First Leeds Wright 'ftr'-bodied Volvo B7LA street car 19023 (YJ07 LVR), with route branding on the cove panels of its front module and its front wheel covers removed. (K. A. Jenkinson)

Arriva West Yorkshire's Optare Tempo 1301 (YJ09 EYB) collects its Castleford-bound passengers on Boar Lane, Leeds, on 9 January 2012. (K. A. Jenkinson)

After its transfer to Transdev Yorkshire Coastliner from Transdev Lancashire United, to whom it was new in April 2007, Wright Eclipse Urban-bodied Volvo B7RLE 1839 (YJ07 PDX) is seen here arriving in Leeds bus station from York on 9 January 2012. (K. A. Jenkinson)

First licenced by Transdev Yorkshire Coastliner in March 2005, Wright-bodied Volvo B7RLE 453 (YJ05 FNM) is seen here in City Square, Leeds, on 9 January 2012, on route 760 to its home base after being transferred to Transdev in Keighley, whose livery it now wears. (K. A. Jenkinson)

New to First Bradford and then transferred to First York, Wright-bodied Volvo B7LA bendibus 10038 (W127 DWX) is seen here in Park Row, Leeds, on 9 January 2012 after moving to First Leeds and gaining a dedicated livery for the 95 service, which connects the rail station with the city's two universities. (K. A. Jenkinson)

Heading along Vicar Lane, Leeds, on 9 January 2012 is White Rose's Centrebus-liveried MCV Evolution-bodied VDL SB180 661 (YJ60 GFO), which was twelve months old. (K. A. Jenkinson)

Seen branded for routes 2, 3, 12 and 13 and their variants, First Leeds barbie-liveried Wright Gemini-bodied Volvo B9TL 37112 (YK07 AYL), which was new in July 2007, awaits passengers in New Market Street in the city centre on 9 January 2012. (K. A. Jenkinson)

Painted in a silver livery and wearing 'Dynamo' branding below its cab window, First Leeds Wright Gemini-bodied hybrid Volvo B5LH 39235 (BP11 JWX), which was new in August 2011, collects its Wetherby-bound passengers in Infirmary Street, Leeds, on 9 January 2012. (K. A. Jenkinson)

Making its way through City Square, Leeds, on 29 November 2012 on the free bus service to Killingbeck Asda, Centrebus Optare Solo M850 274 (YN53 SVE) was new to Northern Blue, Burnley, and then passed to Transdev Lancashire United before reaching its current owner. (K. A. Jenkinson)

Painted in Megabus.com's tenth anniversary livery, Stagecoach Glasgow Plaxton-bodied Volvo B11RT 54201 (SF62 CLV) is seen here picking up its Scottish passengers outside Leeds Minster in Kirkgate on 1 May 2013. (K. A. Jenkinson)

Painted in Bus Eireaan Eurolines livery and seen here in Leeds bus station on 1 May 2013 is Voel, Dyserth's Neoplan N2216SHD Tourliner PJ60 VNF, which was new in January 2011. (K. A. Jenkinson)

Turning into St Peter's Street from York Street, Leeds, on 1 May 2013 is independent Geldards Coaches Optare Spectra-bodied DAF DB250 345 (YJ51 ZVH), which began life with Reading Transport in November 2001. (K. A. Jenkinson)

New to dealers Arriva-DAF, Gomersal, in September 2008 as part of its hire fleet, Plaxton-bodied VDL SB200 YJ58 FFB is seen here passing Leeds bus station on 1 May 2013 while on loan to Centrebus, who had given it fleet number 752. (K. A. Jenkinson)

Despite wearing branding for the airport direct services to Leeds Bradford Airport, Centrebus all-Scania CN94UB 781 (YN03 UVW) is caught by the camera passing Leeds bus station while operating a local service on 1 May 2013 followed by First Leeds Wright-bodied Volvo B9TL 37702 (YJ09 OAW). (K. A. Jenkinson)

Wearing a promotional livery, Transdev Burnley & Pendle's refurbished Plaxton-bodied Volvo B7TL 2706 (B7 BVD, originally Y706 HRN) is seen here on 25 September 2013 operating the Ripon to Leeds 36 service while on loan to Transdev Harrogate & District. (K. A. Jenkinson)

Also new to Transdev Burnley & Pendle in January 2001, Plaxton-bodied Volvo B7TH 2798 (Y708 HRN) is pictured here after its transfer to Transdev Harrogate & District and repainting into a branded livery for the 770 service from Harrogate to Leeds. On 25 September 2013, however, it had strayed onto the prestigious 36 service and is captured in Ripon bus station at the start of its ninety-minute journey to Leeds. (K. A. Jenkinson)

New to Rider York in September 2001, First Leeds Wright-bodied Volvo B6BLE 40576 (YJ51 RSY) travels along Vicar Lane while substituting for an Optare Solo on the free Leeds Citybus service on 8 January 2014. (K. A. Jenkinson)

Passing Leeds United's football stadium on the city's first park and ride route to Elland Road on 19 January 2014 is First Leeds dedicated liveried Wright Gemini-bodied Volvo B9TL 36276 (BD12 TCK), which began life with First Games Transport at the 2012 London Olympics. (K. A. Jenkinson)

Wearing Flying Tiger branding for the services to Leeds Bradford Airport, where it is seen here awaiting its departure to Leeds on 23 October 2014, is Yorkshire Tiger's five-month-old Optare Versa 794 (YJ14 BWY). (K. A. Jenkinson)

Standing on the car park of the Yorkshire Playhouse, Leeds, while undertaking a private hire are independent Geldards coach-seated Alexander-bodied Volvo Olympians L9 YCL and L8 YCL, both of which were new to Yorkshire Coastliner in May 1994. (T. M. Leach collection)

Adorned with Leeds city services Pulse branding and sporting a skyline Leeds fleet name is First Leeds Wright Gemini-bodied Volvo B9TL 36211 (BJ12 VWT), which was new to First Games Transport at the 2012 London Olympics and is seen here in City Square, Leeds, on 23 October 2014. (K. A. Jenkinson)

Starting life in September 1994 as a demonstrator for its coachbuilder, First Leeds Plaxton Verde-bodied Volvo B10B 66652 (M967 GDU) ended its years of service as a driver training bus and is seen here at Leeds railway station on 23 October 2014. (K. A. Jenkinson)

Freshly repainted into Flying Tiger livery, Yorkshire Tiger's ex-Centrebus and Menzies, Heathrow, Scania CN94UB 780 (YN03 UWP) picks up a passenger at Leeds railway station on 7 October 2015 on the 757 service to Leeds Bradford Airport. (K. A. Jenkinson)

Heading along Infirmary Street, Leeds, on 7 October 2015 is Yorkshire Tiger MCV-bodied MAN 12.220 653 (AE57 FBF), which was new to South Wales independent EST Bus, Cowbridge, in October 2007. (K. A. Jenkinson)

Proctor, Leeming Bar's owned Fourways of Guiseley's Alexander Dennis E20D YY64 GTF is seen here on Broadway operating the local Horsforth 30 town service. (T. M. Leach collection)

As is often said, you wait for one and three come together. First Leeds 19023 (YJ07 LVR) heads a trio of Wrightbus Volvo B7LA 'ftr' bendibuses, branded for the Hyperlink 72 service to Bradford, at their terminus in Eastgate, Leeds, on 7 October 2015. This is because, due to their length, they are unable to load their passengers in the bus station. (K. A. Jenkinson)

Arriving in Leeds bus station on 19 April 2016, with its destination already reset for its return journey to its home town, is Transdev in Keighley's Plaxton-bodied Volvo B7TL 2704 (Y704 HRN), which had started its life with Transdev Burnley & Pendle. (K. A. Jenkinson)

Repainted from its original silver livery into First Leeds' new hybrid colours, Wright Gemini-bodied Volvo B5LH 39232 (BP11 JWO) is seen here on Boar Lane, Leeds, on 26 September 2022. (K. A. Jenkinson)

Sporting a 'skyline' fleet name, First Leeds' recently repainted Alexander ALX400-bodied Volvo B7TL 30923 (X791 NWR) is pictured here in City Square, Leeds, on 19 April 2016. (K. A. Jenkinson)

Entering Leeds bus station at 12.29 p.m. on 19 April 2016 is Stagecoach Red & White Megabus. com Van Hool TD927 50239 (CN61 FBA), which was new in February 2012. (K. A. Jenkinson)

Transdev owned 'Harrogate Bus Company' route 36 liveried Wright StreetDeck-bodied Volvo B5TL 3628 (BL65 YZC) arrives at Leeds bus station at the end of its journey from Ripon on 19 April 2016. (K. A. Jenkinson)

PROGRESS Bus Company and seen in Leeds bus station on the 36 service on 19 April 2016 is Wright Gemini-bodied Volvo B7TL 3614 (X14 VTD), which was new to Lancashire United in September 2005 registered PO55 PYP. (K. A. Jenkinson)

Painted in Cityzap livery for the limited stop express service from York to Leeds, Transdev York's refurbished Wright Gemini-bodied Volvo B7TL 3612 (LY03 ZAP) arrives in Leeds bus station on 19 April 2016. New to Harrogate Bus Company in March 2004 registered YC53 MXW, it was later reregistered X12 VTD before becoming LY03 ZAP. (K. A. Jenkinson)

En route to Blackpool on National Express service 351 on 19 April 2016, and seen here entering Leeds bus station, is independent Stott of Milnsbridge's National Express-liveried Caetano-bodied Volvo B9R BK14 LFF. (K. A. Jenkinson)

Painted in the first version of West Yorkshire Road Car Co. heritage livery is First Leeds Wright Gemini-bodied Volvo B9TL 37675 (YJ58 RTX), seen here in Leeds bus station on 19 April 2016. It was given a repaint in this livery in 2022, but on that occasion a narrow cream band was added below the upper deck windows. (K. A. Jenkinson)

In its livery promoting the M-Ticket App, Transdev Keighley Bus Company's Plaxton-bodied Volvo B7TL 2717 (PL51 LDX) is seen here in Leeds bus station on the 760 service to its home town on 19 April 2016. It was new to London General in dual-door format in February 2002. (K. A. Jenkinson)

Passing through City Square, Leeds, on 19 April 2016 is Arriva West Yorkshire Alexander Dennis E20D 1003 (YY14 LFO) sporting the strapline 'little Arriva buses big in Yorkshire' on its side panels. (K. A. Jenkinson)

With Leedscitybus lettering on its front panel and a Leeds skyline fleet name on its cove panels, First Leeds Wright-bodied Volvo B7RLE 66766 (YJ05 VVH) makes its way through City Square, Leeds, on 19 April 2016. (K. A. Jenkinson)

Entering City Square, Leeds, from Park Row on 19 April 2016 is Yorkshire Tiger's ten-year-old MCV-bodied Dennis Dart SLF 548 (AE06 HBX), which was new to Trustline, Hunsdon, in April 2006. (K. A. Jenkinson)

Painted in Arriva's hybrid livery and branded for routes 163 and 166, low-height Wright-bodied Volvo B5LH 1704 (YJ13 FKD) heads through City Square, Leeds, on a journey to Castleford on 19 April 2016. (K. A. Jenkinson)

With route branding and advertising on its cove panels and further route branding at the side of its destination screen, First Leeds Wright-bodied Volvo B7RLE 69416 (YJ09 FXD) enters City Square from Infirmary Street while operating city service 70 on 19 April 2016. (K. A. Jenkinson)

Arriva West Yorkshire Max-liveried Alexander Dennis E40D 1924 (SN15 LLR), with branding for routes 202 and 203 on its lower side panels, is seen here in Leeds bus station on 19 April 2016. (K. A. Jenkinson)

New to Sheffield Mainline in May 1999, First West Yorkshire's Wright-bodied Volvo B10BLE 60665 (T847 MAK) passes through City Square, Leeds, on driver training duties on 19 April 2016. (K. A. Jenkinson)

Seen here in Leeds bus station on 26 September 2022 on the 60 service from its home town, Wright-bodied Volvo B7TL 2758 (PJ05 ZWE) began life with Burnley & Pendle in August 2005, moved to Lancashire United in 2014, and then to Transdev Keighley Bus Company in 2021. (K. A. Jenkinson)

Arriva West Yorkshire Max-liveried semi-integrally constructed low-height Wrightbus Gemini 2 1537 (YJ61 OBM), seen here arriving in Leeds bus station on 19 April 2016, carries branding for Huddersfield to Leeds route 229 on its lower side panels. (K. A. Jenkinson)

Seen awaiting their schoolchildren passengers on 9 January 2017 are independent Square Peg's ex-Arriva Yorkshire Optare Spectra-bodied DAF DB250s T636 EUB and T628 EUB, the latter of which wears branding for the Leeds suburbs 22 service. (Neil Halliday)

Parked on the apron at Leeds Bradford Airport on 12 September 2016 are LBA's five ex-London Mercedes Benz 0530G bendibuses used to transfer passengers between the terminal and arriving/departing aircraft. (K. A. Jenkinson)

Seen on the 72 service from Leeds to Bradford on 4 April 2017 is Pulse-branded First Leeds Wrightbus StreetDeck 35216 (SL16 RGU), which was new in May 2016 and features unglazed front upper deck corner pillars. (K. A. Jenkinson)

New to First CentreWest, London, in May 2003, CT Plus (Yorkshire) Plaxton-bodied Transbus Dennis Trident LK03 NKU is seen here at Temple Newsham, Leeds, operating a schoolbus journey in July 2017. (T. M. Leach collection)

Wearing a branded livery for the limited stop X6 service from Leeds to Bradford is First Bradford Wrightbus StreetDeck 35230 (SL16 YOT), which was new in May 2016. (K. A. Jenkinson)

Seen here with Tetleys Coaches is former Stagecoach East London Transbus Dennis Trident 7830 (LX03 BYD), which is seen here on 21 July 2017 still in its previous owner's livery with fleet names painted out and still retaining its centre doors. (Martin Arrand)

Transdev Keighley Bus Company's Aireline-branded Optare Versa 243 (YJ16 DWM) is seen here on 5 September 2018 in Leeds bus station on the 60 service from Keighley, which was previously numbered 760. (K. A. Jenkinson)

Wearing the new corporate First Leeds livery with added red route branding around the upper deck front, Wrightbus StreetDeck 35289 (SL67 VXT) leaves its stand in Leeds bus station at the start of its journey to Holt Park on 5 September 2018. (K. A. Jenkinson)

Starting life with Burnley & Pendle in February 2009 and moving to the Harrogate Bus Company in 2017, Wright-bodied Volvo B7RLE 1858 (FJ58 LSY) is seen here in Leeds bus station on 26 September 2022 wearing branding for the 7 service to Wetherby and Harrogate. (K. A. Jenkinson)

Painted in the latest version of the Flying Tiger-branded livery, Yorkshire Tiger Alexander Dennis E20D 1072 (YX17 NJZ), which was new in June 2017, awaits its passengers at Leeds Bradford Airport on 16 September 2018. (K. A. Jenkinson)

Seen in Infirmary Street, Leeds, after its evening arrival from Aberford is Connexionsbuses Wright-bodied Scania L94UB YN05 GXD, which had begun life with Reading Buses in March 2005. (Andy Rawnsley)

Arriving in Leeds bus station at the end of its journey from Whitby on 6 August 2022 is Transdev Coastliner's Wrightbus StreetDeck 3635 (BT66 MVU), which was new in January 2017 and, unfortunately from a passenger's point of view, features unglazed front upper deck corner pillars. (K. A. Jenkinson)

Arriving at Leeds bus station on the limited stop X6 service from Bradford on 26 September 2022 is First City of Bradford Wrightbus micro hybrid StreetDeck 35655 (MD71 EOP), which was just seven months old and has glazed upper deck front corner pillars. (K. A. Jenkinson)

Collecting its passengers in York Street, Leeds, at the side of the bus station on 26 September 2022, is Connexionsbuses route 64-branded Scania N94UB YN56 NVG, which was new in January 2007 to Ipswich Buses, whose livery it still wears. (K. A. Jenkinson)

In December 2020, Transdev York & Country upgraded its CityZap fleet with four new dual-purpose-seated Alexander Dennis E40Ds, one of which – 2016 (SK70 WBN) – is seen here on 7 September 2021. (K. A. Jenkinson)

On loan to CT Plus, Leeds, from sister company Powells, Hellaby, Alexander Dennis E20D 1326 (YX11 AEC), which was new to Abellio, London, in November 2011 in dual-door format, is seen here sporting 'Runway' branding at Leeds Bradford Airport on 24 August 2020 after CT Plus had taken over Yorkshire Tiger's contract for the 757 service to Leeds on a short-term basis from 28 June until 2 September 2020, when it passed to Transdev Yorkshire Coastliner (Flyer). (K. A. Jenkinson)

Acquired by CT Plus (Yorkshire) from Lothian Buses, Wright-bodied Volvo B7TL 1990 (SN56 AHD) is seen here in Leeds on 18 September 2021. (Martin Arrand)

Awaiting its passengers in Pudsey bus station on 5 August 2022 is freshly repainted Wright Eclipse Urban-bodied Volvo B7RLE 66996 (YJ07 LWD), which was new to First Leeds in March 2007 and then served for a short time with First York before returning to its original home. (K. A. Jenkinson)

Heading along Broadgate Lane, Horsforth, on 5 August 2022 is Leeds independent Square Peg's Alexander Dennis E20D MX11 JYR, which began life with Padarn Bus, Llanberis, in May 2011 and then served with Mc.Nairn, Coatbridge and Sheffield Community Transport before reaching Leeds in 2016. (K. A. Jenkinson)

Seen operating the final journey through Horsforth on the local 30 service on 5 August 2022 before ceasing trading and going into receivership, CT Plus (Yorkshire) Alexander Dennis E20D 1314 (MX12 DZG) was new to TLC, Bradford, in April 2021 and was then operated by Manchester Community Transport before joining CT Plus. (K. A. Jenkinson)

Turning into Pudsey bus station on 5 August 2022 is First Leeds Wright Eclipse Urban-bodied Volvo B7RLE 69268 (YJ57 YSK), which carries its skyline fleet name on its cove panels to allow space below its windows to be used for adverts. (K. A. Jenkinson)

Sporting orange route branding on its front upper deck panels, First Leedscity Wrightbus StreetDeck 35262 (SL67 VWN) passes through City Square, Leeds, in August 2021 on the 55 service to Cottingley. (Richard Walter)

Collecting its passengers in Pudsey bus station on 5 August 2022 is First Leeds Wrightbus StreetDeck 35260 (YJ70 BHA), which is adorned in Leedscity livery and sports colour-coded grey front upper deck route branding. (K. A. Jenkinson)

Featuring 'R.I.P. HM The Queen – Thank you Ma'am' and route 11 details on its destination screen, First Leedscity dark green front Wrightbus StreetDeck 35578 (SK19 EZG) is seen entering Leeds bus station on 26 September 2022. (K. A. Jenkinson)

Wearing Aireline route 60-branded livery, Transdev Keighley Bus Company Wright Gemini-bodied Volvo B9TL 2794 (X4 VTD) began life in March 2008 registered FJ08 BYN with Yorkshire Coastliner, and then spent some time with Rossendale Transport before moving to Keighley in September 2020. (K. A. Jenkinson)

Painted in a special one-off livery to celebrate its multinational staff, Transdev Coastliner Wright Gemini-bodied Volvo B9TL 2428 (BF62 UXY) moved to Transdev Rosso in 2020 before returning to Coastliner a month before this photograph was taken in Leeds bus station on 26 September 2022. (K. A. Jenkinson)

Entering Leeds bus station at the end of its A1 journey from Leeds Bradford Airport is Transdev Coastliner Optare Versa 239 (Y9 TDV), which was new to Keighley & District in August 2016 registered YJ16 DWF, and was repainted into branded 'Flyer' livery in October 2020. (K. A. Jenkinson)

Arriving at Leeds bus station on 26 September 2022 on its only service to the city – the 116 from Wakefield – Batley-based independent Station Coaches' Wright Eclipse Urban-bodied Volvo B7RLE P2 JJL was new to Longstaffs, Mirfield, in November 2003 and then passed to A. Lyles, Batley, along with its purchase of the Longstaffs operation, before being acquired by its current owner. (K. A. Jenkinson)

Despite wearing the branded livery for First Leeds Temple Green park & ride service, Wrightbus StreetDeck 35301 (SN18 XXW) is seen here in Leeds bus station on 26 September 2022 about to take up a duty on route 28 to the city suburb of Adel. (K. A. Jenkinson)

Adorned in the dedicated livery for the Stourton park and ride service, First Leeds ADL Enviro400-bodied all-electric BYD D8UR-DD 38405 (LG21 HZL) is seen here entering Boar Lane, Leeds, from the Corn Exchange on 26 September 2022. (K. A. Jenkinson)

With navy blue route branding on its front upper deck, First Leedscity Wrightbus StreetDeck 35519 (SK68 TSV) makes its way along Boar Lane, Leeds, on 26 September 2022 while undertaking a journey on the PR1 park and ride service to Elland Road. (K. A. Jenkinson)

Wearing the branded livery for the X84 service to Ilkley, First Leeds ADL E40D 33487 (YX66 WKK), which was new in November 2016, is seen here in Leeds bus station on 22 September 2022. (K. A. Jenkinson)

Repainted into the new Leedscity corporate livery, First Leeds Wright Gemini-bodied Volvo B9TL 37647 (YJ58 RNU), which began life in January 2009, picks up its East Garforth-bound passengers in Boar Lane, Leeds, on 26 September 2022. (K. A. Jenkinson)

Starting life as a Centrebus Flying Tiger bus used on the services to Leeds Bradford Airport before transferring to Arriva Yorkshire in October 2020, Optare Versa 792 (YJ14 BWW) is seen here on 22 September 2022 in Boar Lane, Leeds, on the 163 service to Castleford despite wearing branding for the 167 and 168 services on its side panels. (K. A. Jenkinson)

Arriving in Leeds bus station on 26 September 2022 at the end of its journey from Wakefield on the 110 service, for which it carries route details on its lower deck side panels, is Arriva Yorkshire's Sapphire-branded, three-year-old, low-height Wrightbus Gemini 3 hybrid 1568 (SN69 ZXB). (K. A. Jenkinson)

One of nine Yutung all-electric single-deckers purchased by First Group in September 2020 for its Leedscity operation, 68801 (YD70 CGF) proudly displays its credentials on its side panels and destination screen as it collects its passengers on York Street, outside the bus station, on 26 September 2022, followed by First Leeds conventional Wright Gemini-bodied Volvo B9TL 37650 (YJ58 RNY). (K. A. Jenkinson)

Repainted into Pride livery, First Leeds Wrightbus StreetDeck 35227 (SL67 VXE), with unglazed front upper deck corner pillars, arrives in Leeds bus station on 26 September 2022 at the end of its journey from the city's university district of Headingley. (K. A. Jenkinson)

Seen at their depot in Pudsey, Leeds, on 5 August 2022 are independent Kilvington's ex-Lothian Buses Plaxton-bodied Dennis Trident SK52 OGV and Neoplan coach J26 NTS. (K. A. Jenkinson)

Starting life with Arriva Northumbria in March 2013 and transferred to Arriva Yorkshire in 2018, Wright Gemini 2-bodied Volvo B5LH 1712 (NK13 AZA) is seen here in Leeds bus station on 26 September 2022 after being repainted into Arriva's new hybrid livery, with a green panel below its windscreen and one on the lower deck side, which proclaims its credentials. (K. A. Jenkinson)

Seen en route to Leeds from its home town in August 2022 is First Halifax Wright Gemini-bodied Volvo B7TL 32696 (YJ06 XLO), which was wearing the new HX CONNECT livery. (K. A. Jenkinson)

After its use since new on Transdev Coastliner's York–Leeds CityZap service, ADL E40D 2017 (SK70 BWO) has now been transferred to Transdev Harrogate Bus Company and branded for the X98 and X99 services from Leeds to Wetherby. Here it is seen on 2 October 2022, it's first day in service in its new guise. (Scott Poole)